SPOTLIGHT ON POE

Classic Poems 3

Contents

Collected by Brian Moses and David Orme

COLLINS

Acknowledgements

Whilst every effort has been made to contact the copyright-holders and to secure the necessary permission to reprint these selections, this has not proved to be possible in every case.

'A Storm' by Emily Dickinson, reprinted by permission of the publishers and the Trustees of Amherst College from *The Poems of Emily Dickinson*, Thomas H. Johnson, ed., Cambridge, Mass., USA. The Belknap Press of Harvard University Press, Copyright © 1951, 1955, 1979, 1983 by the President and Fellows of Harvard College; 'Silver', by Walter de la Mare, reprinted by permission of The Literary Trustees of Walter de la Mare, and the Society of Authors as their representative; 'Stopping by Woods on a Snowy Evening' from *The Poetry of Robert Frost*, edited by Edward Connery Latham and published by Jonathan Cape. Reprinted by permission of the Estate of Robert Frost and Random House UK Ltd.; 'There isn't Time' by Eleanor Farjeon from *Silver Sand & Snow*, published by Michael Joseph. Reprinted by permission of David Higham Associates; extract from 'The Highwayman' by Alfred Noyes, reprinted by permission of John Murray (Publishers) Ltd.; extract from 'Night Mail' by W.H. Auden, from *Collected Poems* by W.H. Auden, reprinted by permission of Faber and Faber.

Published by Collins Educational
An imprint of HarperCollins*Publishers*
77–85 Fulham Palace Road
Hammersmith
London W6 8JB

www.**Collins**Education.com
On-line support for schools and colleges

First published 1999

Reprinted 2000

Reprinted 0 9 8 7 6 5 4

ISBN 0 00 310 334 X

Designed by Clare Truscott
Cover Design by Clare Truscott and Kate Roberts
Illustrations by Rob Chapman, Maureen Galvani, Emma Garner, Patricia Linnane, John Lupton, Katty McMurray, Holly Swain, Sarah Warburton, Sue Williams

Printed and bound in Hong Kong by Printing Express

Collins Educational would like to thank the following teachers and consultants who contributed to the research of this series:

Mrs J. Bibby (St Paul's C of E Primary); Jason Darley, Liz Hooley (Jessop Primary School); Mrs M.G. Farnell (High Meadow First School); Alison Lewis; Chris Lutrario; Lesley Moores (Princess Royal Primary School); Sheila Stamp (Castle Lower School); Sally Prendergrast (Brooke Hill School); Jenny Ransome; Jill Walkinton; Sue Webb; Michael Webster (Castle Lower School); Jill Wells (St Andrews CE Primary School).

The Eagle

He clasps the crag with crooked hands;
Close to the sun in lonely lands,
Ring'd with the azure world, he stands.

The wrinkled sea beneath him crawls;
He watches from his mountain walls,
And like a thunderbolt he falls.

Alfred Tennyson

A Storm

An awful tempest mashed the air
The clouds were gaunt and few:
A black, as of a spectre's cloak
Hid heaven and earth from view.

The creatures chuckled on the roofs
And whistled in the air,
And shook their fists and gnashed their teeth,
And swung their frenzied hair.

The morning lit, the birds arose;
The monster's faded eyes
Turned slowly to his native coast
And peace was paradise!

Emily Dickinson

Silver

Slowly, silently, now the moon
Walks the night in her silver shoon;
This way, and that, she peers, and sees
Silver fruit upon silver trees;
One by one the casements catch
Her beams beneath the silvery thatch;
Couched in his kennel, like a log,
With paws of silver sleeps the dog;
From their shadowy cote the white breasts peep
Of doves in a silver-feathered sleep;
A harvest mouse goes scampering by,
With silver claws, and silver eye;
And moveless fish in the water gleam,
By silver reeds in a silver stream.

Walter de la Mare

Stopping by Woods on a Snowy Evening

Whose woods these are I think I know.
His house is in the village though;
He will not see me stopping here
To watch his woods fill up with snow.

My little horse must think it queer
To stop without a farmhouse near
Between the woods and frozen lake
The darkest evening of the year.

He gives his harness bells a shake
To ask if there is some mistake.
The only other sound's the sweep
Of easy wind and downy flake.

The woods are lovely, dark and deep,
But I have promises to keep,
And miles to go before I sleep,
And miles to go before I sleep.

Robert Frost

There Isn't Time

There isn't time, there isn't time
    To do all the things I want to do –
With all the mountain tops to climb
    And all the woods to wander through
And all the seas to sail upon,
    And everywhere there is to go,
And all the people, every one,
    Who live upon the earth to know.
There's only time, there's only time
    To know a few, and do a few,
And then sit down and make a rhyme
    About the rest I want to do.

Eleanor Farjeon

From The Pied Piper of Hamelin

Once more he stept into the street;
And to his lips again
Laid his long pipe of smooth straight cane;
And ere he blew three notes (such sweet
Soft notes as yet musician's cunning
Never gave the enraptured air)
There was a rustling, that seemed like a bustling
Of merry crowd justling at pinching and hustling,
Small feet were pattering, wooden shoes clattering,
Little hands clapping and little tongues chattering,
And, like fowls in a farm-yard when barley is scattering,
Out came the children running.
All the little boys and girls,
With rosy cheeks and flaxen curls,
And sparkling eyes and teeth like pearls,
Tripping and skipping, ran merrily after
The wonderful music with shouting and laughter.

The Mayor was dumb, and the Council stood
As if they were changed into blocks of wood,
Unable to move a step, or cry
To the children merrily skipping by –
And could only follow with the eye
That joyous crowd at the Piper's back.
But how the Mayor was on the rack.
And the wretched Council's bosoms beat,
As the Piper turned from the High Street
To where the Weser rolled its waters
Right in the way of their sons and daughters!
However he turned from South to West,
And to Koppelberg Hill his steps addressed,
And after him the children pressed;
Great was the joy in every breast.
'He never can cross that mighty top!
He's forced to let the piping drop,
And we shall see our children stop!'

When, lo, as they reached the mountain's side,
A wondrous portal opened wide,
As if a cavern was suddenly hollowed;
And the Piper advanced and the children followed,
And when all were in to the very last,
The door in the mountain-side shut fast.
Did I say, all? No! One was lame,
And could not dance the whole of the way;
And in after years, if you would blame
His sadness, he was used to say –
'It's dull in our town since my playmates left!
I can't forget that I'm bereft
Of all the pleasant sights they see,
Which the Piper also promised me.'

Robert Browning

From The Highwayman

The wind was a torrent of darkness among the gusty trees
The moon was a ghostly galleon tossed upon cloudy seas.
The road was a ribbon of moonlight over the purple moor,
And the highwayman came riding –
    Riding – riding –
The highwayman came riding, up to the old inn-door.

He'd a French cocked-hat on his forehead, a bunch of lace
    at his chin,
A coat of the claret velvet, and breeches of brown doe-skin.
They fitted with never a wrinkle. His boots were up to
    the thigh.
And he rose with a jewelled twinkle,
    His pistol butts a-twinkle,
His rapier hilt a-twinkle, under the jewelled sky.

Over the cobbles he clattered and clashed in the dark
inn-yard.
And he tapped with his whip on the shutters, but all
was locked and barred.
He whistled a tune to the window, and who should be
waiting there
But the landlord's black-eyed daughter,
Bess, the landlord's daughter,
Plaiting a dark red love-knot into her long black hair.

And dark in the old inn-yard a stable-wicket creaked
Where Tim the ostler listened. His face was white and peaked.
His eyes were hollows of madness, his hair like
    mouldy hay,
But he loved the landlord's daughter,
    The landlord's red-lipped daughter.
Dumb as a dog he listened, and he heard the robber say –

'One kiss, my bonny sweetheart, I'm after a prize to-night,
But I shall be back with the yellow gold before the
morning light;
Yet, if they press me sharply, and harry me through the day,
Then look for me by moonlight,
Watch for me by moonlight,
I'll come to thee by moonlight, though hell should bar
the way.'

He rose upright in the stirrups. He scarce could reach
her hand,
But she loosened her hair i' the casement. His face burnt
like a brand
As the black cascade of perfume came tumbling over
his breast;
And he kissed its waves in the moonlight,
(Oh, sweet black waves in the moonlight!)
Then he tugged at his rein in the moonlight,
and galloped away to the west.

Alfred Noyes

The Witches' Spell

Double, double, toil and trouble;
Fire, burn; and cauldron, bubble.
Fillet of a fenny snake,
In the cauldron boil and bake;
Eye of newt, and toe of frog,
Wool of bat, and tongue of dog,
Adder's fork, and blind-worm's sting,
Lizard's leg, and owlet's wing –
For a charm of powerful trouble,
Like a hell-broth, boil and bubble.
Double, double, toil and trouble;
Fire, burn; and cauldron, bubble.

William Shakespeare

From King Lear

Blow, winds, and crack your cheeks! rage! blow!
You cataracts and hurricanoes, spout
Till you have drencht our steeples, drown'd the cocks!
...Things that love night
Love not such nights as these; the wrathful skies
Gallow the very wanderers of the dark,
And make them keep their caves: Since I was man,
Such sheets of fire, such bursts of horrid thunder,
Such groans of roaring wind and rain, I never
Remember to have heard...

William Shakespeare

Night Mail

This is the night mail crossing the border,
Bringing the cheque and the postal order,
Letters for the rich, letters for the poor,
The shop at the corner and the girl next door,
Pulling up Beattock, a steady climb –
The gradient's against her, but she's on time.

Past cotton grass and moorland boulder,
Shovelling white steam over her shoulder,
Snorting noisily as she passes
Silent miles of wind-bent grasses.
Birds turn their heads as she approaches,
Stare from the bushes at her blank-faced coaches;

Sheep-dogs cannot turn her course,
They slumber on with paws across;
In the farm she passes no one wakes,
But a jug in the bedroom gently shakes.

Dawn freshens, the climb is done.
Down towards Glasgow she descends
Towards the steam tugs yelping down the glade of cranes,
Towards the fields of apparatus, the furnaces
Set on the dark plain like gigantic chessmen.
All Scotland waits for her:
In the dark glens, beside the pale-green lochs
Men long for news.

Letters of thanks, letters from banks,
Letters of joy from girl and boy,
Receipted bills and invitations
To inspect new stock or visit relations.
And applications for situations
And timid lovers' declarations
And gossip, gossip from all the nations,
News circumstantial, news financial,
Letters with holiday snaps to enlarge in,
Letters with faces scrawled in the margin,
Letters from uncles, cousins and aunts,
Letters to Scotland from the South of France,
Letters of condolence to Highlands and Lowlands,
Notes from overseas to Hebrides –

Written on paper of every hue,
The pink, the violet, the white and the blue,
The chatty, the catty, the boring, adoring,
The cold and official and the heart's outpouring.
Clever, stupid, short and long,
The typed and the printed and the spelt all wrong.
Thousands are still asleep
Dreaming of terrifying monsters,
Or of friendly tea beside the band at Cranston's
    or Crawford's,
Asleep in working Glasgow, asleep in well-set Edinburgh,
Asleep in granite Aberdeen,
They continue their dreams;
But shall wake soon and long for letters,
And none will hear the postman's knock
Without a quickening of the heart,
For who can bear to feel himself forgotten?

W.H. Auden

The Tiger

Tiger! Tiger! burning bright
In the forests of the night,
What immortal hand or eye,
Could frame thy fearful symmetry?

In what distant deeps or skies
Burnt the fire of thine eyes?
On what wings dare he aspire?
What the hand dare seize the fire?

And what shoulder, and what art,
Could twist the sinews of thy heart?
And when thy heart began to beat,
What dread hand? and what dread feet?

What the hammer? what the chain?
In what furnace was thy brain?
What the anvil? what dread grasp
Dare its deadly terrors clasp?

When the stars threw down their spears,
And water'd heaven with their tears,
Did he smile his work to see?
Did he who made the Lamb make thee?

Tiger! Tiger! burning bright
In the forests of the night,
What immortal hand or eye,
Dare frame thy fearful symmetry?

William Blake

Jabberwocky

'Twas brillig, and the slithy toves
    Did gyre and gimble in the wabe;
All mimsy were the borogroves,
    And the mome raths outgrabe.

'Beware the Jabberwock, my son!
    The jaws that bite, the claws that catch!
Beware the Jubjub bird, and shun
    The frumious Bandersnatch!'

He took his vorpal sword in hand:
    Long time the manxome foe he sought –
So rested he by the Tumtum tree,
    And stood awhile in thought.

And as in uffish thought he stood,
    The Jabberwock, with eyes of flame,
Came whiffling through the tulgey wood,
    And burbled as it came!

One, two! One, two! And through and through
    The vorpal blade went snicker-snack!
He left it dead, and with its head
    He went galumphing back.

'And hast thou slain the Jabberwock?
Come to my arms, my beamish boy!
O frabjous day! Callooh! Callay!'
He chortled in his joy.

'Twas brillig, and the slithy toves
Did gyre and gimble in the wabe;
All mimsy were the borogroves,
And the mome raths outgrabe.

Lewis Carroll

Upon Westminster Bridge

Earth has not anything to show more fair:
Dull would he be of soul who could pass by
A sight so touching in its majesty:
This city now doth, like a garment, wear
The beauty of the morning; silent, bare,
Ships, towers, domes, theatres, and temples lie
Open unto the fields, and to the sky:
All bright and glittering in the smokeless air.
Never did sun more beautifully steep
In his first splendour, valley, rock, or hill;
Ne'er saw I, never felt, a calm so deep!
The river glideth at his own sweet will:
Dear God! the very houses seem asleep;
And all that mighty heart is lying still!

William Wordsworth

Glossary

The Eagle
crag steep, high rock
azure blue

A Storm
tempest powerful storm
mashed shook violently
gaunt grim-looking
spectre ghost
gnashed ground together
frenzied wild
his native coast the coast of his own country

Silver
shoon shoes
casements windows
thatch a roof made of straw
couched lying
cote home for doves

Stopping by Woods on a Snowy Evening
downy like a feather

From The Pied Piper
ere before
enraptured overcome by magic
fowls hens
flaxen fair
on the rack in a very difficult situation
Weser the river that runs through Hamelin
portal doorway
lame disabled
bereft without

From The Highwayman
cocked-hat an old-fashioned three-cornered hat
claret red, the colour of wine
breeches trousers
butts the part of a pistol held in the hand
rapier hilt sword handle
cobbles stones used to make a road
stable-wicket stable door
ostler person who looked after horses
press me sharply chase me
harry hunt
though Hell should bar the way even if devils from Hell try to stop me
stirrups rider's foot-rests
scarce barely
i' old-fashioned spelling of 'in', used to help the rhythm
brand burning torch

The Witches' Spell
toil hard work
fillet something that has had its bones removed
fenny from a marsh
owlet baby owl

From King Lear
cataracts waterfalls
wrathful angry

Night Mail
border boundary between two countries
postal order way of sending money through the post

gradient a steep climb
apparatus equipment
furnaces steel-making factories
lochs Scottish word for 'lakes'
receipted send with a receipt
applications for situations job applications
lovers' declarations love letters
news circumstantial gossip
condolence regret that someone has died
Highlands and Lowlands the two parts of Scotland
Hebrides Scottish Islands
hue colour
Cranston's or Crawfords Edinburgh restaurants
granite a hard stone used for building

The Tiger
immortal living forever
thine your
aspire reach as high as possible

sinews heart-strings
dread feared
furnace fire for turning ore into metal
anvil metal platform for shaping metal tools
Lamb young sheep, or a symbol of Jesus

Upon Westminster Bridge
doth does
garment item of clothing
ne'er never, shortened for the rhythm

Index of poems by title

Index of poems by first line